Ringed by Language.
And Yet.

Justy Phillips

Justy Phillips is an artist and writer who grew up in the soft green fells of the north of England and now lives and works on the banks of timtumili minanya in nipaluna/Hobart, lutruwita/Tasmania. She is co-founder with Margaret Woodward of A Published Event, a collaboration forged through shared acts of public telling. A graduate of the Royal College of Art, London, Justy holds a PhD from RMIT University, Melbourne. Her writing can be found in the form of essays, books and architectural text-works. In 2019, Justy was awarded the Ruth Stephan Fellowship at the Beinecke Rare Book & Manuscript Library, Yale University. Justy's publication Fall of the Derwent was long-listed in the 2017 Premier's Literary Awards, Tasmania, Australia. Her work is held in public and private collections internationally.

Justy Phillips

Ringed by Language.
And Yet.

First published in Australia in 2022
by Upswell Publishing
Perth, Western Australia
upswellpublishing.com

Copyright © 2022 by Justy Phillips

The moral right of the author has been asserted.

ISBN: 978-0-6452480-3-6

A catalogue record for this
book is available from the
National Library of Australia

Cover image: watercolour by Ilana Halperin,
Fields Studies (from Kilchattan Bay to Hawk's Neb) 15,
courtesy of the artist and Patricia Fleming, Glasgow.
Cover design by Chil3
Typeset in Foundry Origin by Lasertype

At first I see only darkness and then the silhouette. Matte black and immobile, I join its lines into a shape that appears as two-dimensional horse.

After a few seconds, illuminated momentarily by a passing silver-grey sedan, its score of distended ribs etches diagonal lines into the back of my late-night eyes. A lone, emaciated horse standing on a highway in Tirana. I am transfixed, not by its absent light-dead body but by the backlit landscape of its standing. Yellow-green light from a nearby apartment block hangs from concrete edges, drawing the shape of the horse's undercarriage into the horizon of an imaginary mountain.

So quiet and so still is this air, that I almost do not feel its violence. Drifting in and out of focus, he and I share lines of fuzzy concrete that blur his standing into mine, intermittently.

It is unusually quiet on this highway. Has someone doctored the sound? The intermittent crease of distant automobiles and muffled hounds do nothing to soften my concern. For its welfare.

After a few minutes, another car, this time with horn blaring and blister-white headlights. Only now do I see the horse balancing precariously on just three legs. The fourth, a rear hind leg, it calls quietly up and into its light-filled mountain-scape.

Time and again, my view is obscured by passing trucks that suck the horse's image out of sight. And then back again. Vacillating abstractions, feathers underfoot. This is the violence. This threshold that is not-yet. Rigid, I plead. Please don't fall. Grip my hands and synchronise my breathing to the horse's wavering leg. *Please don't fall.*

What I really want to say is please don't fall while I am watching.

What is failure? / incalculable / breathing ground /
tender white heart of a cabbage / indivisible /
metamorphosis / glass-blown lungs / the orbits /
out of time / gall bladders more valuable than
gold / the possibility of touch / touching itself /
latency / societies of living holes / some leg
weakness / what is a heart? / vermillion shuddering
/ to be always already full / the seat of life / and
albeit rarely used / of memory / to be present /
when all else is all else / that infinite touch of
nothingness / must be a gift / as Moten says, to feel
the feel / what else? / I think I was born this way.

I am eight years old when my legs first fall from under me. It happens in the field adjacent to our house. The field where our chickens sleep. Peck scattered corn from dark brown soil. I remember his coarse nylon trousers. The broken lining of his pocket. Crystalline, friable, acute. I remember that we did not stop moving not even as hands passed under clothing. I remember looking at the ground, thinking how careful you must be to navigate the little mounds of corn feed and shit. Thinking how far you would need to dig.

In all the years that have passed, I have wondered
if my faltering legs that did not rest that morning,
knew already that a leg is also a heart. Knew already
that what falters on the ground never begins there.

If I were a rock or blood sea, I might drill out this heart and flood it with something more spectacular. More capable. A new kind of touch. Perhaps some place for the goldfinches to return. I would pay more attention. Be more aware of beats that slip away through fingertips, plumage and shin. Mouth open to brackish water. *I would take more care.*

Beneath the surface, I would swim the grounding lines, a vast system of blood vessels—arteries, veins, capillaries, eel pits and crab dens. For sixty thousand miles I would roam, circumnavigate the organs, slip between the tips of bleaching coral. If I were a pool of crimson blood, or even a glass of it, I would draw the world in sanguine lullaby. Break the lips of every verse with segments of sharp winter orange.

Twelve months ago I was diagnosed with congestive heart failure. I am forty five years old.

I knew it in myself the previous year, somewhere in that vast shoreline of rock and sea. Last summer I felt my chest tighten. In autumn, rapid changes in the colour of my skin, as oxygen, in tiny increments, found it harder to reach. Winter brought leg weakness and dizzy spells. Intense afternoon fatigue in spring.

Heart failure, caused by a diseased and weakened heart muscle, leaves one unable to pump enough blood to meet the needs of the body. *The needs of the body.* When the heart is unable to distribute blood effectively, fluid begins to accumulate in the blood vessels, eventually leaking into the space around the lungs and other areas of the body, causing shortness of breath and swelling. With each beat, less oxygenated blood is ejected from the heart, eventually starving the muscles and organs of the nutrients they need to survive. Submerged. Altering. This body that is nearly drawn. *Full of bite.* And the pigment of fresh water.

I am twelve years old.

A champion of sorts and already one of England's fastest young swimmers.

Steadying myself to enter the warm Mediterranean Sea of the Costa Brava, even I am unsure. Surface chopping soft peaks from dark water. My mother's slender body, rising from a river of hot-golden-corn-drenched-sand, assures me that I can make it.

The pontoon is tethered some way out but is surely less than the daily looping circuits of our municipal pool. I can feel my pulsing leg-heart draw something down and into that field of shifting sand but I never let my eyes fall from the water. *Never let go of that swim.*

A sea of bodies close to shore. And then nothing. Just me and the nasty grip of all that water. From the surface, everything looks close. *The gate. His shoes.* And yet the pontoon, with each stroke. Still and still beyond my reach.

The coastguards are called at great expense. Still outbound, my adolescent body about to unfold. I am lifeless. I hold out my arms as they haul my limp frame into the boat. Scold me one by one for what is seen as reckless. My cold skin catching on seams of welded rubber. My gasping chest. The noise of the motor. The wind. Pale legs. And all that water. This is how we live our grief. In risk. *Otherwise we are only half-living.*

Back on the beach, my mother looks sheepish. Thanking the coastguards in broken Spanish she uses one arm to close her body into me. With the other, she turns us gently away and up the beach to the shade of our umbrella. I know she is disappointed but about what I'm not exactly sure. That I hadn't made it all the way to that small floating island or that its refuge was only a mirage of something it should have been. Years later she tells me that she was embarrassed at having encouraged me to go into the water that day, and that she lied to the coastguard when they questioned what I was doing all the way out there, in that corn-scattered field of dark water. *Pushing jellyfish from my arms.*

When I tell you that every heart is always already a shared body, is always already entangled, you will understand that every failing heart is a complex social body too. Heart failure is more than a physical entity; it is a body of work, a movement, an idea. A throbbing force of living memory.

An accomplishment.

Neglect. Amnesia. Will.

In Berlin, I board a train for Moscow. The Steppes, Kazakhstan, Uzbekistan, Turkmenistan. I go alone. I am nineteen years old. *It will be years before I will let anyone really touch me.*

Months earlier in a London waiting room, I see an image of rusting hulls stranded in the sands of the Aral Sea. I want to know how it feels to be held in that waterless basin.

In the grip of winter it takes three weeks to reach the site in the western reaches of Uzbekistan. I am reckless. Take many more risks than are necessary. With access prohibited to foreigners, I lie my way in. And then I hide in the shadows of a blistering sun and everything that is stranded in that place bleaches me. Peels back skin after skin. *The way that jumpers are pulled from the bodies of small children.* What burns my eyes moves too quickly to nip or scratch. Fugitive. In the distance, the mirage of something. *A mother. A pontoon. Salt water.*

A body should not need to be performing daily activities dependent on emergency systems. 'Pull the emergency brake', they say. Nobody moves. Some leg weakness. I think I was born this way. Two and a half thousand miles from home, anchored like Gulliver to the sands of that cancerous, dry lake, I am overwhelmed. *Bantams scratch the ground as I am moved.*

Memory. Time. Stutter. Shunt. And then. What is seized. Thrombosis. Cavity. Core. There is no sound at all. Glass eels in endless bodies of murky water. Driven by salinity and odour. *It takes years to discover what was already gone.*

In the city of Samarkand, I hear an English voice in the Siyob Bazaar. He is tall. Robust. Grew up on a Riverina wheat farm. Everything about him is quiet and soft. I suggest he join me on my journey to the empty sea. We are tourists. Before such a thing takes hold in this place. En route we stop in Khiva, a town encircled by sweeping tenth century walls and night as soft as what cannot be said. What follows as skin comes to skin is trapped in thick, raw silence. *Sorry.* This man. All tender hands. Me, a grief-stricken child.

This is just the beginning. The panic. Paralysis. This is the wound that will come to glaze every tiredness. Out there in the midday sun where nobody is watching. And here in the thickening chambers. *A calcifying stomach full of plastic.* I fold back into myself. Send my blood to rush his veins ahead of me. With every kindness, every intimate touch, my body returns me to the fizzing loop of what I did not see coming. Vagrant. Convivial. This fugitive-chronicle. See now how all the tongues move in the telling.

When did all the wounds come together and announce themselves as one? *Was I there?*

In a converted Weslyan Chapel in the north of England, three pairs of arched windows on the north, south and east span walls of ashlar stone. Inside, a three quarter turn staircase sweeps our small family from vestibule to choir loft through Hornbeam. Rowan. Ash.

Ankle-deep in rivers of hand-made parquet flooring, my father, an artist, spends long days replacing great panes of broken nineteenth century glass. In his absence my mother does her best to care for her children in the vast, unheated worships of this place.

By the time I am three, their union is over. My father moves to a cottage in nearby woods, buys a pair of Belted Galloways. And another man moves in.

My mother remarries quickly. A sister is born. And somewhere in that fog a man who gardens and mends things is employed. *A man whom I adore.* Until I am spent. And all that love is stunned by a tight grip and a certain way of holding.

Believe me when I say. You can drown just looking at all that water.

Jellyfish. At first in rings. And then desire. When the heart's electrical system becomes diseased, signals can get blocked causing the left ventricle to contract a fraction later than it should. This partial dissociation causes hearts like mine to permanently shake. To wobble. Coursing electrical waves leak out from the circuit. Activating surrounding tissue. Electrifying the body in a permanent state of arousal.

When I first glimpse my body hugging the spindles
of those wild chapel stairs, I am seven or eight or six.
Thick as clay. I am all gut. Thoracic. My mother and
step-father wrestling over and over, marrying some
kind of tidal darkness down below.

There is no beginning to their violence. Just this
image on the stairs. Bodies moving up and down the
small vertical staves of pre-flight. No punches are
thrown but wrists are sprained. Bodies are marked.
And broken. Clinging to the risers. Eye level with the
choir. A Mouth. Ringed by language. *The circle's out
there in plain sight on the water.*

What is in-bracing? Does it hurt?

When it is over, that long and terrible walk to feed the chickens. I say what I can to my mother. I begin with his name. Push it quickly at her body so that she too feels the force of it. All at once.

Trying desperately to surface the shape of my distress, I inhabit what is empty. What is left. *Rattling sponges from their rest.* I ready my mouth. Let my tongue give shape to what is taken. The capture. The salinity. The dirt. With my body I try to say. *Drawn in broad daylight and then and then and then.* And yet, something tells me this is not what I said.

At the kitchen table, my small frame feels completely rigid. Does my mother reach for me? Pull me close? In my moving-not-moving I feel only the air from her voice as it makes, over and over, the mouth shape 'everythingwillbealright'.

In this moment, I am elated. Vindicated. I have never been more certain of anything in my life.

When it is impossible to say. How much time has elapsed between kitchen table and now. My mother takes my hand and leads me to 'a surprise' in the garage. At first I just catch a glimpse, mid-construction, of a spectacular home-made fancy dress costume. A solid prism of deep-purple-walkable-cake split into two perfect halves with reams of back and forth, horizontal cotton wool. And then, emerging slowly from inside the timber framework, I see *him*.

One by one my ribs fall inward. Forfeit what is gathered. A pilot whale swallows seventeen pounds of plastic bags in local waters. Fishing nets. Packing straps. Fifteen rice sacks. Gloves and plastic tubing. Its stomach acid, unable to break down the plastic waste, wears holes through its stomach lining instead. *Mitral regurgitation present.*

Some place quiet. Away from here. My mother tells me that he has been reprimanded. This man who they employ as gardener, handyman, friend. *Failure is mutable.* I watch her push the words towards me. *All at once now.* 'It won't happen again'.

I should have said the word hunger or ragfish or organs or shell. I should have made the mouth-shape of holding or held. I should have said ribcage or weight or fin or scale or skin. I should have said inside. And accumulate.

As what is held again collapses. I understand that I am believed. But now I can't be sure. Of what I said or when I said it. Only that I did not say enough. *You are not enough.* I turn myself inwards. And then to the pool. How that deficit lingers.

If I had known it then, I might have recognised this swelling not as weakness, but as time folding back on itself. This creature of the failing heart, not a failure of the body but of the ways a body might come to experience itself.

Send me a line that simply reads: *You are kind and gentle.*

In the safety of my mother's womb my heart grows well. Begins to falter, only when I am separated from her body. What should close a few days after birth, in my small frame, refuses. A congenital defect between the two upper chambers of a heart. With each heartbeat, already oxygenated blood escapes the atria, returning instead, and again, away from the body. Through shimmer and lung.

Twenty years from now this hole, that is more absence than perimeter, will be the size of a walnut. *This hole that nobody knows is growing.*

In a field full of chicken shit and daylight.

Eyes wild and bracing. I know at least there will be an end. I know enough before this happens to understand it will hurt.

With the trees approaching at rapid speed, my brother lets go of my waist and tumbles into the soft snow behind me. Seconds later, I am splayed like an octopus in spines of shattered spruce. I am seven or six or eight.

My forehead splits. Takes the impact of collision as the yellow plastic sled skims the hill without me. I am cracked wide open, releasing great surges of thick, red blood into the snow. And then relief. This leaking. This trickling away. And all I can think is that it is possible. To escape from this body. This bed of sawdust and stinging nettles. *This field.*

In the impact, I am motionless. Quiet. Mouth ensnared in woody flesh. Hair in plated bark. Only now, as I am pulled from scattered limbs, do I feel the sound of what is held. And then the wool coat of my mother.

With the weight of my child body slumped across her chest I watch as more and more of my insides leak out, pooling first in my mother's woollen shoulder. And then the snow.

The ground turns to slush beneath her as I am turned, forehead first towards my stepfather. I know what is coming but there is no language. No mouth-feel. To meet this terror.

I understand that I am about to be touched at the same time as being held. I am paralysed. I try to free myself from my mother's arms, kicking wildly at her knees. Her response is to grip me tighter so that my stepfather can get close enough to hold together with one hand, all the edges of my wound. If I could speak this moment. I would say.

You are not safe. Not here in my mother's arms. Not here in the park. Not here in my stepfather's surgery. Not here in the sutures that he is weaving so carefully in and out of my resistance. You are not safe in this body. *Not anywhere.*

When the needle finally enters with its single
thread casting back and forth between us, I do not
feel it. I feel only the pressure of being moved.
I tell myself. You are water.

And yet. Feel nothing at all.

It begins with a passing touch on the back of my head. *Ankles tight, not yet swelling.* Arms that reach up and over from behind. In need of a hammer. A bag of screws. *Chest pressure. Sore eyes. Diaphragm collapsing.* Hands that rest. And press and push and hold and part. Make clear a path that is visible to no one and nothing. This threshold that is not-yet rigid. And still, displaces the air. *Weakens the walls of the pumping chamber.* Until it no longer has the strength to empty each time, what is filled.

This is the violence.

Afferent fibres carried towards. In shallow, laboured breaths. As if to say. *What is gone is gone.* Now you must learn to absorb what follows.

When you are medicated, drugged, it is impossible to remember.

Beta blockers open arteries, give my heart a chance.
Difficulty sleeping. Dizziness. Fatigue.

In Rocky Cape, Newfoundland, a female blue whale crushed by sea ice washes ashore. Hers is the first heart of this size in history to be preserved through plastination. It takes five men to carve a window into the flesh and push her heart clear of the thoracic cavity.

Once you decide to shape a thing this way, there is no going back. A swimmer's body is for life. I am not sure if I fully understand this at the time. When I am twelve.

In the water I am alone. I am safe. Quiet. Strong.
I am no longer a girl but something *other*. A whisper.
A thought. A deception.

Up and down the pool, I feel the shape of water shaping me. Its mutable body pressed against the outline of my skin. Mostly it is thin like glassine. And some days it actually dissolves. This rare occurrence, when skin is no longer a stomach full of plastic nor a blush of garden fruit. *But a glitch in the Universe.* This is when I am sure. When all the thresholds are gone. I am a body of water from plumage to shin. Eel pit. Blood sea. Crab den. Stop.

When I am not dissolving, which is most of the time, when I am a body that kicks and pushes and gasps for air, I am thinking. I feel my heart beating in my back, reaching outwards through the cross straps of my costume. And with this rhythm, between the mouthfuls of air, I hum to myself or run through my homework for the day. Before school, I swim these lines onto sheets of paper. Tumble. Repeat.

With every second breath I catch a glimpse of my coach, striding poolside, his hands flapping wildly to indicate that I should use my legs. This kind of pressure helps one remember. *Just how far you need to dig to stay afloat.*

Sometimes I count my breaths. Breathing bilaterally, my body moves in symmetry with the water. This is important to me because buoyancy can be so difficult to achieve. I develop a pattern of breathing that enables me to see equally, all sides of the body. Sometimes I see my coach. Sometimes a mother or a father arranged up and down the tiered stone seating.

Usually, I take a new breath every five strokes, but sometimes I run to seven, nine, fifteen. Even with a hole that nobody can see, I can hold my breath longer than almost every one of my team mates. Almost two lengths of these stone baths. *I shape my arms like flinted arrows and kick and kick and kick.* Until I am tired and everything hurts again.

Each day I tell myself, this has to come to an end.

Rigid in a sea of rainbow clowns, I am standing with my classmates on the road outside my school. I am eight years old. Dressed as a slice of cherry sponge.

I watch them laughing, touching, reaching for each other's brightly coloured hair. Inside, I am composed. Quiet. Surrounded completely, by the edges of my poster-paint-acrylic-wadding-desert.

As the teachers usher us in turn towards the line, I quickly walk my fingers around the inside of my cake. Pick up the frame that is invisible to the parents who line the pavement on each side, invisible to the faces of my classmates.

When the whistle blows the other children start to run. Lunging forwards. Heads out wide. I have practiced for this moment. In the garage, in the long hours after school. Me, and the gardener who built this slice. That I am now wearing in front of everyone. My mother decorated the outside of *his* construction, attaching sheets of beautiful purple tissue for layers of sponge and swathes of cotton wool for sandwiched cream. Its weight, the culmination of what I must have seemed able to carry.

I tighten my grip. Move my legs that did not stop that day. Propel my body forwards.

There is no doubt in anyone's mind that mine is the most exceptional creation. And if moving were not a requirement of this race, I am sure I would have won. By the time I reach the finish line, my shins, that have with each step forward been held uncomfortably by the inside of that wooden frame, are red and swollen. *We are all exhausted.* And what should have been so much fun is too much. Even for me.

I remember how red my cheeks felt, how the sweat ran down the sides of my face. Under my tee shirt and down the inside of my chest. We hadn't factored in the incline. How difficult it would be to carry all that weight ahead of me. When I could finally let go, my arms would not stop shaking. 'You were magnificent', said my mother, 'You should have won'.

Osiris. God of the dead: Water darkens everyone.

Midway up the garden, a patch of gooseberry snares morning sun. Planted by my stepfather but tended to by *him*. Cooling properties of acid juice in fevers. Pies. Jellies. Fools. *It must be after ten*. Transparent skin tones mimic dense panes of nineteenth century chapel glass. Each time I think, this is a perfect fruit. Until the hairs.

All I remember is silence. *But I know this is not what I heard.*

When I am still a child my father moves back home with his parents. No television. No fridge. No electrical appliances at all. My grandmother doesn't want that kind of pulsing through her home. And I don't blame her. This is an artist's house which means you can see everything the artists want you to see.

The house is full of sculptures. Near naked bodies in flight. *Men who use their hands for something beautiful.*

Alongside her studies at the Royal Academy of Arts in London, my grandmother began assisting her father, the artist Charles Sykes in casting hundreds of editions of his Spirit of Ecstasy. In 1908 his 'Silver Lady' was adopted as the official mascot of the Rolls Royce Motor Company. I grow up knowing that the body is something to be handled. In the private moments of a home. *In broad daylight.* At dad's house, the silhouettes are everywhere. At my house they are shadows torn from wallpaper. Until I use my own saliva to carefully glue them back in place. It is a long time before anyone notices their edges. Misaligned but holding.

The stairs are lined with mascots and casting moulds,
female bodies partially clothed in various positions.
Outstretched. Breasted. On their knees. Pots
crammed with brushes and carving tools.

From the window, frog spawn, the careless spill
from yesterday's too-hot afternoon. Over and over,
the cardiac contractions of a pithed frog's heart,
sutured to the bitumen. *Spit. Hold.*

Twice a week and then three times and later, four,
I swim for one hour in the pool before school. We
call it morning training. I am eleven years old, and
later fifteen.

My mother drives me there and back and, when I am
flushed, bleached with chlorinated water, we return,
wake my brother and sister and I eat breakfast all
over again.

Some days I do not make it to school at all. Or I make
it and then I leave at midday, walking home for the
lunch that my mother leaves for me on a porcelain
plate in the fridge. A stomach full of cold-sliced beef
and tomatoes that she cuts into interlocking stars.
After lunch I skip the afternoon's classes. English
Literature, History, Cross-country running. Instead
I work the whole afternoon from the kitchen table,
thinking, drawing, gluing strips of newspaper into
papiér mâche bowls.

At home I smell my chlorine-comfort-skin everywhere. In the carpet, the cutlery, the cuts of meat. It is a smell that returns me to myself. *Suture.* Some days, embedding myself in this aroma of chemical soaked water is the only way to find the edges of my body. When its shape is already blurred or what's left. Dissolving. I lick the back of my hand, release its germ-killing acid. Bring it inside. Some kind of bleaching. *Where all the vibrant colours turn to white.*

In all the years that I have been licking my skin. *I don't think that anyone has noticed.* I am careful and calm. I begin by holding my hand close to my face. In one move I run my tongue along the skin between knuckles and wrist and then move the wet skin to my nose. The chlorine has an instant bite. It is so quick. The sensation. And then the relief.

Mostly I lick my skin when I'm at school. When I am fractured by the smell of upset—an atmosphere of sweet-meal biscuit. A body pressed too long into stale carpet.

Do not wrap yourself in mouth-feel. For it is everywhere. And then it is nowhere at all.

I am unsure how this tenor makes my body disappear. This smell that paralyses me in the corridor. The classroom. The queue for the dining hall for the toilet for the bell. This smell that is layers and layers of unwashed clothes and eating tea at five o'clock. It is poverty with mouthfuls of nylon. And yet I can't say this or this or this. I have no language for my knowing for my skin for this smell. That is reaching. That is always one step ahead.

I do not tell a soul about this fracture. Instead I say 'I am tired' or 'I hate school' or 'It's boring' or 'I have no friends', all of which are true and also not true. This way I do not have to think about the smell of school, that I do not yet understand as *memory*.

We visit my father when we can.

Mostly we go by train. Unaccompanied, with money for chocolate and cans of fizzy drink. A week at a time. Beyond the canals and mill towns of the South Pennines. We sing to each other. Until the bastard countryside gives way.

I see the outline of my body, held upright on the ground. Blades of grass reach from brown-black soil. Others flounder, arching backwards from the earth, where careless boots hold them under. Turn them inside out.

It must be after ten. The sun, snared in sheet-grey sky is interrupted now and then by the slender cut of chimneys down the valley. One after another, the woollen mills flatten. A foreground of excretions. In green and white and tan. Trauma is a pressure made of air. Now a breeze. Remember how it feels. To be stilled.

I don't breathe, not then. And yet my mouth must have opened itself. To bite it all up. This folded-folding time. That is pressing years of awkward holding all at once. Time bolts inside itself. And still I cannot move. Cannot push apart our bodies. Cannot break myself in two.

If I tell you there was language, I do it only to
stabilise myself. Perhaps to hold myself to account.
Glossolalia. There is none. I do not hear a thing.
I cannot even make the word string. Fluke. Blubber.
Sap. Sting.

Efferent fibres carried away. Bites of something
certain. Becoming indistinct. Failure enters every
part of me. Begins to dissolve. And what is felt is
slant and crude. *Until it is nothing at all.*

It is not what I thought remembering would feel like.
This hunger of weak legs and tongue.

On my twelfth birthday, my father arrives with a plan.

We will walk to the top of the nearest mountain. This is something he can manage. And somehow we will need to manage too.

Dressed in summer shorts, I join my brother and sister in the back of Dad's ageing car. Bare legs peel thighs from vinyl seats as we turn to wave our mother. Her diminishing presence too soon disappears, *as patches of muscle tear pale salmon to red*. In the driver's seat, my father's head fills completely. The dark silhouette of Schiehallion.

I do not know it yet but I will come to hate these kinds of hills. The ones with false summits. Clawing your way to the top only to find it is just another edge. Just a fragment of something bigger. A deception. *Braeberry. Heather. Stale cigarettes.*

After hours of silent climbing we are surrounded by thick, cold fog. Dad reassures us over and over that we are 'nearly there'. But now there's a boulder field and zero visibility between us and the peak. I would like to say that final scramble was too much for my sister, but perhaps it was too much for me.

Legs already gone. Either way, Dad tells us to wait by this cairn while he takes my brother to the top. In a split second they are invisible. Ask the rocks. We are alone. My sister and me. Howling wind. *Then nothing.*

We will taunt him for years, my father. In front of anyone who will listen. Remember when you lost us up that mountain? What we really mean to say is, *remember when you lost us*. It is not a question. But a mourning. I am thinking now how much it can hurt to say one thing when you mean another. To confuse language with love.

In the eighteenth century, Schiehallion, with its near perfect conical form, was the site of an experiment to determine the mean density of the Earth. None of us know this at the time. *And if my father knew, he never said.* It was all to do with the gravitational attraction of the mountain. They had pendulums and quadrants. We have an orange and each other. When I make the decision to descend without them, I have my sister's frozen fingers in one hand and a fistful of skin in the other.

We scramble back down the rock field, she and I, placing small stretches of peel on every cairn. Above us, on the far side of the mountain, my brother and father are finally reunited. Everything is white. I do not let go of her hand.

Just before we reach the car park, Dad's voice breaks through the wind. 'I've got him. I've got him'. My relief is swamped. *Why did no one think to go looking for me.*

In the evenings when Dad take us with him to the pub because we are too young to leave at home, he fills his bones with malted ale and we three sink the bitter memory of that hill into the smooth folds of our studded leather barstools. In these soft hours he is even more gentle. Captive. Time and again we find some way to remind him, draw his shame like an arrow, of how he left us in the grasp of all that quartzite scree. What we don't say. Can't say. Is how that dense and irrecoverable mountain was already inside us. *Was already inside me.*

You put a glass of water on the table. You think it's doing nothing. But its always looking for a way out.

When I am eight and before that, five and six and
seven, I spend all my free time in the garage of the
chapel, building useful things out of scraps of wood.
My first best thing is a small chest of drawers, nailed
together from off-cuts I salvage from the local wood
yard and then cover in burgundy corduroy from the
rag bag. Lining up furrows of fabric with the
straight edges of my timber brings me pleasure and
when it is firmly glued in place, I instinctively run
the back of my hand up and over the newly softened
ploughs of my box. *I think this is when it begins.*
My coercion. What is safety? Does it hurt?

Each morning and night and all the quiet times
between when I am gripped by inseparable tiredness,
I roll up the sleeve on my right arm, turn my radius
inwards and drift my skin up and down the cool,
smooth surface of my cotton duvet. I make myself
known over and over to the margins. Not a single
day goes by without me reaching, in this way, for
the thresholds of my skin.

Winter is the best. Followed by long shoulders of autumn and spring when the air is still tempered. It is true that in summer, it is more difficult, more confusing, to establish with this method, the outer limits of a core. Even now, most days, I like to carefully create the conditions for contact—pull the duvet tight in the morning, scatter touch-appropriate furnishings in all the reaches of our home. A smooth, cool surface gives immediate relief. Too many creases or folds, plate shifts of any kind (leaking sunlight, clothes left mindlessly on the bed) cause ruptures, even slight. In the service of a body, it is near impossible to locate one's skin in the disruption of sedge and spume.

For years, my confidently clad chest of furrowed skin has pride of place on top of an actual chest of drawers in my mother's bedroom. She fills it with so many precious things that before long the drawer can no longer be closed. And yet, the corduroy continues to absorb all these particles of light and dust and other people's touch. *Breasts. Heart. Lungs. Pleurae. Tracheobronchial tree.*

When I first hear the news. That my heart is leaking, I feel something grip deep inside. Its not the absence nor the edges-that-can't-hold. It's the idea. Beyond experience. That the hole was always already there.

From the day I was born to the day I am thirty. *It grows as I grow.* It is one of the largest holes they have ever seen, they say. And so quiet compared to all the others they have ever heard. They stand in turn with their heads to my chest and no one is allowed to breathe. Except me. And no one can hear its unusual shape. Except me.

When the hole in my atrium wall is finally repaired, my heart remains unsure of how to control its own activity. It has many workarounds. Looping relays. Something addled. Indivisible. *If I didn't already know the earth was curved, I never would have seen the arc at all.*

I endure two rounds of radiofrequency ablation in an attempt to correct my heart's arrhythmia. These procedures involve long wires being passed into the heart through a vein in the groin. Energy, in the form of heat, is passed through the wires to modify the heart tissue, destroying those parts of the muscle that trigger or sustain abnormal heart rhythm. *Tiny pieces of my heart burn in situ.*

Cardiac ablation requires the patient to be sedated but not completely anaesthetised. *I am told I won't feel a thing.* But it's not true. I feel the hum of moving bodies. The vibration of voices as the nurses and other technicians talk in loud tones about last night's television shows. I feel the wires move inside my heart. Feel the red-hot heat of scar tissue forming. *A tripwire held in place.*

The first time I have this procedure, several disorganised electrical rhythms are successfully ablated. At the age of thirty-five, my atrial fibrillation is corrected and my heart returns to normal rhythm. This heart that was always-already entangled, suddenly feels strong. I am elated.

Within a year, the abnormal conduction fibres have regrouped elsewhere causing new interruptions, flutters and speeds. The procedure is repeated. The same medical team drift up and down my body, but the new groupings can't be found. As they work, I feel this mass of blood and verse sink to the ocean bed. Pulses of soft flesh gather. Ratfish. Hagfish. Burrowing worms. Lab-induced whale fall.

I am wheeled into recovery. I have failed to make felt what happened before and before and before, leaving mounds of labile matter, stranded on the cath lab floor.

How seismic it is. This terror.

At thirteen I stop talking. For three whole weeks
I find a way to shed the wicking beds. That are
every place but the water. These grounding lines
that I have tethered so defiantly to the people that
I love, I pull from their flesh one by one. For the
first time I control what can be seen. Turn their
eyes on me.

My mother is beside herself. My swim coach
puts his arm around my shoulders. Which I like.
I have the power now. Make them come to me.
And it is terrifying.

I tell myself, you will remember this moment for
ever. But I don't. I can't say it happened on this
day or that, in this pool of water or that. Millrace.
Ocean. Inland sea. Just that it is over.

I push my teenage body up and over the stone-
lipped pool. Heavy. Empty. Spilling what is left.
What is left? I run my fingers through my hair.
Pinch my nose and blow until there is nothing.
I watch my body move ahead of me. Legs that
carry, one last time this out-of-water weight
towards the showers. I am completely undone.
Shoulders burning. *What is memory? Does it hurt?*

I don't look back. I can't look back. In the water
I am tight and pale. I am whole. What repels in
there, is suddenly forgotten. Beached. I steady
myself. It's over.

For seven years I have spent more time in the pool than almost anyone else I know. I am saturated. Fingertips pulsing smooth, wet granite as I exhale what is lost into a stream of lukewarm water. Look at me now. I am just shapes again. Lungs. Shins. Plumage. Toes. *What remains.*

I speak to my coach. Over. And over. Try to reconcile achievements against loss. But somewhere in the last few laps of this evening's training session, I finally accept that every lap, every breath, every race— none of this will be enough. To recover.

I steady myself. Let the chlorine settle. And now the shock: I still cannot find the outline of my body. I cannot say it is this or this or *that*. I used to think, if I can do this. If I can just keep going.

Winter fruit. Clothes removed. *Or not at all.*

When he is too busy cutting staves of walnut and elm into box-sized pieces in his workshop, my father places us in the care of someone else. We spend these days roaming the fells with a trusted friend who runs an outdoor education centre off the moor.

It is the one thing that nobody tells you. When you enter a hole in the earth. A crease in the heather. That you will be held in uncomfortable ways.

Lying on my belly. Dead weight in rushing water. The wet is some kind of overwhelming darkness. Voices echo. Head torches illuminate in a way that nothing can be seen clearly or remembered as it was. The cave is ice cold and black, revealing only one truth. You will not find pleasure in the struggle. In the company of adults, you will not be able to say. I am terrified. A limestone pavement swells chronic touch. *Cough while lying down.*

At first the freezing cave water is expelled by protective clothing, but as the stream shallows and the ceiling lowers, smooth boulders trace a belly full of organs from below. I try not to panic. *Diaphragm in spasm.* But as the water finds its way out of the cave and through the protection of my outer layers, permeability comes as something stunned. Otherworldly. And that mineral seam floods in.

When I am thirty eight years old, an implantable
loop recorder is inserted into my chest. Embedded
in the muscle of my left breast. This stranger
records the electrical activity of my heart, enabling
its remote monitoring over the next three years.
Every quiver, impulse and confused swell is
transmitted in real time to my doctor. No one knows
it is here, this thing that records everything. But for
the scar and the sometimes mound of its foreign
body. It is invisible.

At the push of a button my device can instantly
recall the last three minutes and capture the next
three minutes of my life. A loop of memory. And
with it I use my heart to divide *something indivisible.*
Duration. Continuity. Plain sight.

My back hurts all the time.

The deterioration begins at the base of my spine.
What rushes in, snaps upriver. Doctors ask me, did
you fall. Did you turn awkwardly? And I think no.
I didn't move at all. It hurts when I stand too long or
sit too long. When I stretch in any direction. The
outline of my body. It is chronic. This pain that is
made of time. *Of being moved.* Through childhood.

In all those circuits of the pool, the water helps but
still, the pain licks my bones like a grieving tongue.
Adrift and yet. People say.

For pain relief, rub this cream on the muscles, place
this wheat pack on the bones. But it's deeper than
that. It's memory wrapped in gill tissue.

I am seven or six or eight years old when my legs
first fall from under me. It happens in a house
beyond the field. Sun-cracked midday curtains.
Melting shafts of yellow into gold. I remember the
weight of his hand on my neck. The smell of my
mouth. The close-cut tufted carpet pressing into the
back of my head. I remember thinking. This will
hurt. And then, through open legs, I see the
silhouette of both men. What is solid is also
dissolved. One is on top of me. Inside me. The other
is watching. Making ready his turn. My organs.
A seizure of burnt umber and sharp winter orange.

Quietly. Awkwardly. And then in pain. I am touched.
Sedated. Immobilised. Held in unprecedented ways.
With heavy, lifeless limbs I am lowered onto
concrete. Pressed onto unfamiliar linen. I am
undressed. Handled. Bathed.

Dead soft lead. What is cast over and over, quickly
re-marks all the edges. Spoon sinker. Surface. Core.
I try to discern what is inside and out. What is
outline. What is depth. Time. Sponge. And yet, in
the incomplete wound of memory, I find myself
unable now to tell you how it feels. To be touched.
How it feels to be present in that delay.

In the water column, small particles begin to gather. Tiny fragments at first and then, in broad daylight, a gyre. You ask yourself, what does it take to salvage a heart? To bring it back. What is altered, polarised. What is lost in the glare. Continuity. The field. The lounge room floor. *A failing heart might last five years. Six, seven, eight, nine.*

And now I am thinking. There won't be enough time. *To be held.*

Acknowledgements

Without this particular heart, faltering as it is, it is unlikely I could have written the other inseparable vessel of the past. It is clear to me now that they are not two individual things, these durations, but the ongoing threshold of one intelligent, fizzing thing. Perhaps this is how it is to write a heart. In part, painful and confusing. And yet, it surprises me each day that even in the wake of such terror, the heart remains, somehow. Full of love.

To those of you impacted by the trauma of sexual abuse in childhood, I want to thank you for being with me here. I acknowledge with deep empathy the unspeakable difficulties of our particular kinds of trauma and gently move myself alongside you.

And to my first and closest readers, who have somehow absorbed with their own bodies the impact of what happened to me. You have made possible this body of writing. This creature. These mouthfuls of air. More than anything, I now understand, that this, *this* is the trying.

The title of this book was prompted by the words of artist Brandon LaBelle, whose extraordinary book *Lexicon of the Mouth* presents this vessel as an organ *ringed by language*. And yet, for me, it all remains so difficult to say.

I am extremely grateful to Ilana Halperin and Patricia Fleming Gallery for permission to reproduce Ilana's stunning artwork for the cover of this book. This watercolour on Fabriano Paper is #15 in the series *Field Studies (from Kilchattan Bay to Hawk's Neb) 1–36*, (2019). I cannot think of a more accurate skin through which to invite you into this writing than the densely folding pleats of this study.

Several passages in this book first appeared in Meanjin Quarterly in the layers of my essay, *What We Cannot See* (Volume 80, Issue 3 Spring 2021). I gratefully acknowledge the editors and publisher of Meanjin Quarterly for extending their platform to this emerging voice.

To artist Roni Horn, I am indebted to your vision of the Arctic Circle beyond its ocean skin. Anchored here on page 33: *The circle's out there in plain sight on the water,* and page 86: *If I didn't already know the earth was curved, I never would have seen the arc at all.* See Horn, R. (1991). *Pooling Waters / Vatnamot: I Can't See The Arctic Circle From Here.*

To my fearless publisher Terri-ann White and the team at Upswell Publishing, thank you for finally making public what has been private for so long. And to Ross Gibson and Sian Prior for showing me the way. I extend my heart to NK, WM and KDV for holding me close as I pass through that overwhelming threshold from there to here. And finally, to MW, the love of my life. Thank you for choosing me.

About Upswell

Upswell Publishing was established in 2021 by Terri-ann White as a not-for-profit press. A perceived gap in the market for distinctive literary works in fiction, poetry and narrative non-fiction was the motivation. In her years as a bookseller, writer and then publisher, Terri-ann has maintained a watch on literary books and the way they insinuate themselves into a cultural space and are then located within our literary and cultural inheritance. She is interested in making books to last: books with the potential to still be noticed, and noted, after decades and thus be ripe to influence new literary histories.

About this typeface

Book designer Becky Chilcott chose
Foundry Origin not only as a strong,
carefully considered, and dependable
typeface, but also to honour her late
friend and mentor, type designer Freda
Sack, who oversaw the project. Designed
by Freda's long-standing colleague,
Stuart de Rozario, much like Upswell
Publishing, Foundry Origin was created
out of the desire to say something new.